The Believers Code

The Believers Code

WINNIE M SMITH

RMKI PUBLISHING / DIVISION OF ELLIE MEDIA INC

Copyright © 2021 All rights reserved.

NO PART OF THIS PUBLICATION MAY BE REPRODUCED, STORED IN A RETRIEVAL SYSTEM, OR TRANSMITTED IN ANY FORM OR BY ANY MEANS, ELECTRONIC, MECHANICAL, PHOTOCOPY, RECORDING, OR ANY OTHER, WITHOUT THE PRIOR WRITTEN PERMISSION OF THE AUTHOR

This book was produced with Pressbooks (https://pressbooks.com) and rendered with Prince.

Contents

Foreword — vii
Acknowledgement — ix
Introduction — 1
PREFACE — 6

Part I.

1. THE BELIEVERS CODE — 9
2. THE DOCTRINE OF SALVATION — 13
3. THE OLD AND NEW TESTAMENT — 26
4. INTRODUCTION TO CHRISTIAN LIFE — 36
5. A TREE RECOGNIZED BY ITS FRUIT — 51
6. WARNING FROM ISRAEL — 59
7. JESUS HEALS ON THE SABBATH — 64
8. THE HIDDEN SECRET OF A HAPPY LIFE — 76
9. HOW IS IT ACCOMPLISHED — 83
10. REFLECTIONS — 89
11. THE FALL OF MAN: THE NATURE AND FINAL CONSEQUENCES OF SIN — 103
12. GOD'S GREAT COMMISSION FOR HIS PEOPLE:IS THE COMMAND TO "PRAY" — 116
13. TESTIMONIALS — 118
14. SCRIPTURES FOR NEW BELIEVERS — 121
15. DAILY INSPIRING AFFIRMATIONS FOR YOU TO RECITE — 124

ABOUT THE AUTHOR

Foreword

I want to thank the Lord for the life of Prophetess Winnie Smith and for using her mightily in teaching, healing, deliverance, and the prophetic.

For six years, I have seen Prophetess Winnie Smith grow in faith, love, healing, and deliverance. She is a humble woman of God, always caring for others and helping those in need. I have never seen her compromise her word; she always stands for what is true.

Prophetess Smith is a woman of faith and wisdom, and I admire her faithfulness to the Lord. I thank the Lord for using Prophetess Smith to write such a brilliant book, which contains a profound revelation that will help all believers walk with the Lord.

The Believer's Code is an anointed book full of great insights, knowledge, and wisdom. It contains many nuggets and powerful teachings to help you grow in your relationship with God. The Believer's Code is a must-have; This book truly blessed me.

Apostle Johnny Albert

General Overseer and founder of Kingdom Builders Tabernacle

KBT School of Deliverance, KBT Prophetic School, and KBT School of the Prophets.

Acknowledgement

I want to give honour, glory, and majesty to my Lord and Saviour Jesus Christ for calling me out of darkness and into his marvellous light. He has shown me supernatural revelations from a young age because he had grand plans for my life. I thank God for my parents, Zephaniah the Prophet, whose mother was Prophet Jane Williams, and Amy Williams, who was from a Prophetic Gene. She had the gift of Prophecy; her dad, my grandfather, was "Prophet Emmanuel Geohagen," who had planted the seed in my siblings' and my lives. I give thanks to my loving five children. Andrea, my second child, went home to be with the Lord in 2012, along with Donovan, Marvin, Makini, and Desiree. I want to acknowledge Pastor Richard and Pastor Taba Pena from Christ Embassy, located at 77 Ingram Drive, North York, Ontario, where I became a member of their Church, led by the Spirit, in December of 2018. They are the actual demonstration of God's love in the lives of His children.

Thanks again, Pastor Richard and Pastor Taba, for allowing me, through the spirit of

God, to demonstrate my gift of Prophesying in the Church! I would also like to acknowledge Prophetess Victoria A. Morgan, with whom I joined her mentorship group in 2019. Being accountable for completing my solo book, I faced challenges in scheduling my goals and finding the time to discipline myself to move this project forward. Still, after joining this group, I was able to accomplish most of the writing through fasting and prayer.

To Apostle Johnny Albert, who had been a true mentor in my life! Apostle Johnny had taught lessons in the School of the Prophets. Deliverance profoundly and miraculously, I have seen deliverance demonstrated in such a way that only God can demonstrate His power to his children whom he has called and chosen. We had been into homes to deliver to families and bless their homes. God has placed an Apostle in my life for the past 6 years, serving as a mentor for the calling upon my life! As a healing and deliverance Prophetess/Apostle.

Thanks again, Apostle Johnny, for allowing

me, through the spirit of God, to demonstrate my gift of Prophesying in the Church! I would also like to acknowledge Prophetess Victoria A. Morgan, with whom I joined her mentorship group in 2019. Being accountable for completing my solo book, I faced challenges in scheduling my goals and finding the time to discipline myself to move this project forward. Still, after joining this group, I was able to accomplish most of the writing through fasting and prayer.

To Apostle Johnny Albert, whom God divinely placed in my life many years ago as a mentor for the calling upon me. As a healing and deliverance Prophetess/Apostle, I honor him for being the only Prophet who consistently spoke accurate prophecies over my life — from the womb to my childhood and beyond. He has seen the things the Lord has spoken concerning me, even the things hidden from others. I give him the utmost respect because he is a true MOG, one who speaks the mind of God with purity and precision. The Bible says…

"For many are called, but few are chosen"

(Matt. 22:14)KJV I give God thanks for the privilege of meeting Apostle Bible Davids and his loving wife Prophetess Rebecca Bible Davids during such a time of the pandemic season, who also speak into my life and see the strength and anointing of God upon my life! I give Him all glory and honour.

Introduction

God created us in this world for a purpose; So God created man in his image, in the image of God created he him; male and female created he them. (Gen. 1:27)KJV God is purposeful in everything he does; He orchestrated his creation. The earth is the Lord's and the fullness thereof; the world and they that dwell therein.

For he has founded it upon the seas, and established it upon the floods. Who shall ascend into the hills of the Lord? Or who shall stand in his holy place? He that hath clean hands, and a pure heart, who hath not lifted his soul unto vanity, nor sworn deceitfully? He shall receive the blessings from the Lord, and righteousness from the God of his salvation. This is the generation of them that seek him; that seek thy face, O Jacob. Selah!

I can attest that I was one of the chosen ones! Set apart, sanctified, cleansed and purified, but it was difficult to submit to the call; it took many in-and-outs. An adversary out there fought me for a while to stay focused and humbled in God. I want you to know that God's choosing process is different; many are called, but few are chosen!

Faith, obedience, endurance, and commitment to God will see you through tough times. I present this book with the teachings and the process I endured, knowing how God intended believers to live. God has equipped me and given me a specific task: to heal and deliver His people.

See, I have set thee over the nations and kingdoms, to root out and pull down, destroy and throw down, build and plant. Jeremiah 1:10, I hope this book will encourage and bless you.

Prayer:

It is one command God requires from us; it is necessary. We know that there is an adversary out there; Satan is roaming the earth seeking to destroy all that he can take! The Bible says; Be sober, be vigilant, because your adversary the devil walketh about as a roaring lion, seeking whom he may devour.

1 Peter 5:8 KJV "THE THIEF COMETH NOT, BUT TO STEAL AND TO KILL, AND TO DESTROY." (John 10:10)KJV

I am come that they might have life, and that they might have it more abundantly; I am the good shepherd: the good shepherd the good shepherd gives his life for the sheep vs;11 But he that is an hireling, and not the shepherd, whose own the sheep are not, seeth the wolf coming, and leaveth the sheep, and fleeth; and the wolf catcheth them, and scattereth the sheep vs;12 The hireling fleeth, because he is an hireling, and careth not for the sheep, vs;13 I am the good shepherd, and know my sheep, am known of mine. vs;14

Fellowship and communion with God involve adoration, worship, praise, thanksgiving, supplication, petition, confession, repentance, meditation, dedication, and intercession.

Christian prayer is addressed to God as Father through and in the name of Jesus Christ, his Son, and is based on the confidence that he hears from his children. Prayer is drawn partly from the urgency of human needs and partly from the promise and challenge of God's Word. The awareness of God's presence shapes personal prayer. Corporate prayer is the living breath of the Church.

Through prayer, the Church resists Satan's assaults. Watch and pray, lest you be tempted. The spirit is indeed willing, but the flesh is weak.

(Matt. 26:41; Eph.6:13-20); receives the gifts of grace (Acts 4:31); 2 | Introduction

seeks deliverance, healing, and restoration for the saints (Eph. 6:18; James 5:15; 1

Support evangelism and hasten the return of the Lord. (Rev. 22:20). Let your light shine before men, that they would see and glorify the Lord. Matt.5

Withal pray also for us, that God would open a door of utterance, to speak the mystery of Christ, for which I am also in bonds. I may make it manifest, as I should speak.

Walk in wisdom toward them that are without, redeeming the time. Let your speech always have "GRACE" seasoned with salt, so you may know how to answer every man. All my state shall Tychicus declare unto you, a beloved brother, and a faithful minister and fellow servant in the Lord: Whom I have sent unto you for the same purpose, that ye might know your estate, and comfort your hearts. (Col, 4: 3-8)KJV

PREFACE

The Believer's Code is a foundational guide for every Christian who is serious about understanding how God intended His people to live. Drawing deeply from Scripture, prophetic insight, and years of ministry experience, Prophetess Winnie M. Smith brings forward a powerful, uncompromising teaching on spiritual growth, sanctification, biblical doctrine, and the lifestyle standards expected of a faithful follower of Christ.

This book demystifies critical theological principles — salvation, justification, sanctification, spiritual warfare, and the fruit of the Spirit — breaking them down in a way that is accessible yet spiritually rich. Through detailed studies of Old and New Testament truths, Smith outlines how believers are to walk in obedience, holiness, and unwavering faith in a world filled with compromise.

At its core, The Believer's Code is a blueprint for Christian living. It reveals the "codes"

God has established for His people: the code of conduct, integrity, love, forgiveness, perseverance, resilience, virtue, and spiritual discipline. Each chapter equips readers with biblical tools to stand firm, live righteously, and recognize the enemy's traps through sound doctrine.

With strong prophetic undertones and practical application, this book challenges readers to examine their hearts, grow in spiritual maturity, and live out their identity as God's chosen vessels. It is both a manual for new believers and a refresher for seasoned saints who desire depth, clarity, and alignment with God's original intention.

Whether you are pursuing deliverance, strengthening your prayer life, or seeking to understand who you are in Christ, The Believer's Code offers transformative teachings that illuminate your path and call you to higher ground.

This is not just a book — it is a spiritual training ground. A preparation. A call back to God's standards.

Perfect for:
- ✓ Church discipleship programs
- ✓ Bible study groups
- ✓ Personal devotion
- ✓ Deliverance and prophetic training cohorts
- ✓ Christian leaders seeking doctrinal clarity

1. THE BELIEVERS CODE

How God intended for His people to live

"If any of you lack wisdom, let him ask God, who gives generously to all without reproach, and it will be given to him." (James 1:5) NASB God is Sovereign and ever-knowing. He is El Shaddai, "God Almighty." He is the God of good and plenty. He has created the Earth and everything on it.

Gen. 1:1-5 KJV; 'In the beginning, God created the heavens and the earth. 2. And the earth was without form, and void; and darkness was upon the face of the deep. And the spirit of God moved upon the face of the waters. 3. God said, Let there be light: and there was light. 4. God saw the light as good: God divided the light from the darkness. 5. God called the light day, and the darkness he called night, and the evening and the morning were the first day.

The day is thine; the night also is thine: thou hast prepared the light and the sun. (Psalms 74:16) KJV

(Psalms 74:16) KJV We see in scripture the prophecy of the forerunner! Who has directed the spirit of the Lord, or being his counsellor, has taught him? (Holy Spirit) With whom did he take counsel, and who instructed him, taught him in the path of judgment, knowledge, and showed him the way of understanding? (Isaiah 40:13-14) KJV

These biblical references are great for studying and learning God's true insights. As believers, we should have a clear understanding of the process, and many will have gotten a clear picture of how God has planned his ways in our lives.

No Christian can take from this book; it is the genuine revelation of how we should live for God when we are born again. Therefore, if any man has been in Christ, he is a new creature: old things have passed away; all things have become new. (2 Corinthians 5:17) KJV

SOTERIOLOGY:

The study of the Religious Doctrine of

SALVATION – NOUN: THEOLOGY:

It is the systematic study of the divine nature of GOD AND RELIGIOUS BELIEF. God's attributes and relationship to THE UNIVERSE: GOD IS A SPIRIT; HE IS INFINITE, ETERNAL, AND UNCHANGEABLE IN HIS BEING. — NOUN

ship to THE UNIVERSE: GOD IS A SPIRIT; HE IS INFINITE, ETERNAL, AND UNCHANGEABLE IN HIS BEING. — NOUN

2. THE DOCTRINE OF SALVATION

Where the salvation is assured to them, has been delivered from the wrath of God destined to be executed upon the ungodly at the end of this age, see (1 Thess 1:10) KJV And to wait for his Son from heaven, who he raised from the dead, even Jesus, which delivered us from the wrath to come. (2 Thess. 2:13) KJV says, but we are bound to give thanks always to God for you, brethren beloved of the Lord, because God hath from the beginning chosen you to salvation through sanctification of the Spirit and belief of the truth. (Gen.1:14) KJV says, And God said, let there be lights in the firmament of heaven to divide the day from the night and let them be for signs.

1 Pet. 1:5 We see those who are kept by the power of God through faith unto salvation, ready to be revealed in the last time. (Pet. 3:15); But sanctify the Lord God in your

hearts and be ready always to answer every man that asketh you a reason for the hope in you with meekness and fear. (e.g.) of the deliverance of the nation of Israel and the second advent of Christ at the time of "the epiphany, A holiday which is a Christian feast day that celebrates the revelation of God incarnate as Jesus Christ. (Theophany)

Another name for people in the East; it refers to a deity manifesting in a visible form. (Or shining forth) of His Parousia" (2 Thes. 2:8); And then shall that Wicked be revealed, whom the Lord shall consume with the spirit of his mouth, and shall destroy with the brightness of his coming.

(Luke 1:71) KJV We should be saved from our enemies and all those who hate us. KJV; In the AMPC: Says, "That we would have

THE DOCTRINE OF SALVATION | 7

deliverance and be saved from our enemies and from the hand of all who detest and pursue us with hatred." For as much as many have taken in hand to outline a declaration of the things most surely believed among us.

(Rev. 12:10); KJV "And I heard a loud voice saying in heaven, Now is come salvation, and strength, and the kingdom of God, and the power of Christ: for the accuser of our brethren is cast down, which accused them before our God, day and night.

To some up all the blessings bestowed by "GOD ON MEN" in Christ through the Holy Spirit, see, 2 Cor. 6:2-4 scripture says: For he saith, "I have heard thee in a time accepted, and in the day of salvation have I succored thee: behold, now is the accepted time; behold, now is the day of salvation. vs. 3, Not offend anything, that the ministry be not blamed" vs. 4, But in all things approving ourselves as the ministers of God, in much patience, in affliction, in necessities, in distress.

Heb. 5:9; 1 Peter 1:9; 10; Jude 3; (e.g.) occasionally, as standing virtually for the saviour. Let's look at the NIV. In verse two, he says, "In the time of my favour I heard you, and on the day of salvation I helped you. (Luke 19:9) NIV And Jesus said unto him, "This day is salvation come to this house, as he also is a son of Abraham." (John 4:22) KJV Ye worship ye know not what: we know what we worship: for salvation is of the Jews. (Rev. 7:10) NIV "and they cried with a loud voice: "Salvation belongs to our God, who sits on the throne, and to the Lamb." and as that which it is His prerogative to bestow, 19:1; (KJV); And after these things I heard a great voice of much people in heaven, saying, Alleluia; Salvation, and glory, and honor, and power, unto the Lord our God.

We bow down and worship the king of "GLORY" because he is Holy. We praise him for all he has created on the earth; hallelujah! He is God, all by himself, and nothing is impossible for him to do.

8 | THE DOCTRINE OF SALVATION

God also lets His people know when He is about to do something; He speaks His mind to His prophets, and He doesn't do anything until He reveals it to them. He speaks of his anger for the people; he intends us to get it right!

The name of the book speaks volumes, it explains how the Father wants His people to live on earth; when he doesn't get his ways, he will send wrath upon the land, God is a forgiving God, a faithful God, a God of righteousness; Holy is he that sits on the throne, he is Omniscient, the ever knowing, all wise God. He is Omnipresent, the God who is everywhere, at all places at all times, giving him glory! Hallelujah. The Omnipotent God: Having unlimited power, he can do anything.

Sorter on the neuter of the objective, is used as a noun in Luke 17:30; And the times of this ignorance God winked at; but now commandeth all men everywhere to repent; Luke 17:3-4, Take heed to yourselves: If thy brother trespass against thee, rebuke him; and if he repents, forgive him. vs. 4; And if he trespasses against the seven times in a day, and seven in a day turn again to thee, saying I repent; thou shalt forgive him. In each of which it virtually stands for the saviour (e.g.)

(a) (Acts 28:28) KJV Be it known therefore unto you, that the salvation of God is sent unto the Gentiles, and that they will hear it. (b) In Eph. 6:17, where the hope of "Salvation"

(c) It is metaphorically described as "a helmet" and takes the Helmet of Salvation, and the sword of the Spirit, which is the word of God: see Ephesians 6:10-18 KJV "Finally, my brethren, be strong in the Lord, put on the power of his might."

Put on the armour of God that ye may be able to stand against the devil's wiles. For we wrestle not against flesh and blood, but against principalities, against powers, against rulers of darkness, of this world, against spiritual wickedness in high places. Wherefore

take unto you the armour of God that ye may be able to withstand in the evil days, and having done all, to stand. Stand therefore, having your loins girt about with truth, and having on the breastplate of righteousness; and your foot shod with the preparation of the gospel of peace; Above all, taking the shield of faith, wherewith ye shall be able to quench all the fiery darts of the wicked. (And take the helmet of salvation, and the sword of the Spirit, which is the word of God); Praying always with all prayer and supplication in the

Spirit, and watching thereunto with all perseverance and supplication for all saints. OH, YES! The Bible explains it here: "PRAYING ALWAYS." Believers need to pray, rejoice evermore, and pray without ceasing! In everything give thanks. For this is the will of God in Christ Jesus concerning you.

1st Thess 5:16-18 KJV Adjective: "saving, bringing salvation" describes the grace of God.

SANCTIFICATION:

- Verb Word 'Qadash' means to sanctify, "be holy" in the primary stem; the verb signifies an act whereby, or a state wherein people.

- Things are set aside for worship of God: they are consecrated or "made sacred." By this act and in this state, the thing or person consecrated is to be withheld from workaday use (or profane use) and treated with exceptional care as a possession of God. Exod. 29:21 KJV And thou shalt take of the blood that is upon the altar, and of the anointing oil, and sprinkle it upon Aaron, and upon his garments, and his sons with him: and he shall be hallowed, and his garments, and his sons' garments with him. There are also overtones of ethical and moral

10 | THE DOCTRINE OF SALVATION

(spiritual) holiness here, as the atoning blood was applied to the people involved. The state is emphasized when the word is used in Exod. 29:37 KJV In some cases, we see here: Seven days thou shalt make an atonement for the altar, sanctify it; and it shall be the most holy altar.

- Whosoever toucheth the altar shall be holy.

- "Set aside for GOD," MEANS DESTRUCTION, 2 Sam . 6:6, 7. KJV And when they came to Nachon's threshing floor, Uzzah put forth his hand to the ark of God, and took hold of it; for the oxen shook it. And the anger of the Lord was kindled against Uzzah; and God smote him there for his error; and there he died by the ark of God; While in others it means such things are to be used only by those who are ritualistically pure, Num. 4:15 KJV And when Aaron and his sons have made an end of covering the sanctuary, and all the vessel of the sanctuary, as the camp is to set forward; after that, the sons of Kohath shall come to bear it: but they shall not touch any holy thing, lest they die. These things are the burden of the sons of Kohath in the tabernacle of the congregation.

- These things are the burden of the sons of Kohath in the tabernacle of the congregation.

- In the passive stem, the verb means "to prove oneself holy," Num 20:13. This proving refers not to an act of judgment against ethical-moral holiness. But a miraculous act of deliverance. Another emphasis is to be treated as holy, as seen in Isa. 5:1; Deut. 6:3ff.

- Qadash can mean "to declare something holy" or to declare it to be said exclusively to celebrate God's glory (Exod. 20:8) or a pagan God (2 Kings 10:20). The word comes to mean "to

declare" and make proper preparation for war (Jeremiah 6:4; cf KJV). Prepare ye war against her; arise, and let us go up at noon. Woe unto us! The day goes away, for the shadows of the evening are stretched out.

- Mic . 3:5; (NIV) This is what the Lord says: As for the prophets who lead my people astray, they proclaim "peace" if they have something to eat, but prepare to wage war against anyone who refuses to feed them. NIV; Thus, saith the LORD concerning the prophets that my people err, that bite with their teeth, and cry, Peace; and he that put not into their mouths, they even prepare war against him. Mic. 3:5 (KJV) Jeremiah 51:27; NIV; Lift a banner in the Land! Blow the trumpets among the nations! Prepare the nations for battle against her; summon against her these kingdoms: ARARAT, Minin and Ashkenaz. Appoint a commander against her; send up horses like a swarm of locusts. NIV; KJV; Set up a banner in the land, Blow the trumpet among the nations! This stem may also put something or someone into a reserved state.

- Prepare the nations against her: cause, call the kingdoms together against her: Ararat, Minni, and Ashkenaz; Appoint a general against her; causes the horses to come up like the bristling locusts; exclusively for God to use, Exod. 13:2; NIV, Consecrate for me every firstborn male. The first offspring of every womb among the Israelites belongs to me, whether human or animal. NIV; KJV Sanctify unto me all the firstborn, whatsoever opens the womb among the children of Israel, both of man and beast: it is mine vs. 12-13; KJV; You are to give over to the Lord the first offspring of every womb. All the firstborn males of your livestock belong to the Lord. Redeem with a lamb every firstborn donkey, but if you do not redeem it, break its neck. Redeem every firstborn among your sons. NIV: "That thou shalt set apart unto the LORD all that openeth the matrix, and every firstling that cometh of a beast which thou hast; the males shall be the LORD'S 13. And every firstling of an ass thou shalt redeem with the lamb; and if thou wilt not redeem it, then thou shalt break his neck: and all the firstborn of man among thy children shalt thou redeem.

1 Sam. 1:24. NIV; After he was weaned, she took the boy with her, young as he was, along with a three-year-old bull, an ephah of flour and a skin of wine, and brought him to the house of the Lord at Shiloh. (NIV)And when she had weaned him, she took him up with her, with three bulls, one Ephah of flour, and a skin of wine, and brought him to the house of the LORD in Shiloh. (KJV)

- Qadash may also be used to make something or someone cultically pure and meet God's requirements for purity in persons or things used in the formal worship of Him. This Act appeared in Exodus. 19:10. Although the primary emphasis here is ritualistic, there are ethical morals. God directed Moses to have the artisans make special clothing for Aaron. Exod. 28:4.

3. THE OLD AND NEW TESTAMENT

SATAN-THE OLD TESTAMENT

"Adversary; Satan." This word has two explicit references: (a) an evil being who is the opponent of the true God, Job 1:6-12; 2:1-7; (b) A human being who opposes God or another human. Ps 38:20; 71:13; Ps. 109:4; cf. also 2 Sam. 16:5ff. God can also be the "adversary." When Balaam went to curse the Sons of Israel, God warned him not to do so. When the prophets persisted, God disciplined them (Num. 22:22); with Solomon, 1 Kings 11:14. One must carefully read in some contexts to decide who the "Satan" or "Satan" is, but in the New Testament, it nearly always refers to the person of Satan.

SATAN- THE NEW TESTAMENT

A Greek form derived from the Aramaic (Heb.) Satan, "an adversary," is used (a) of an angel of Jehovah in Num. 22:22, the first occurrence of the Word in the OT (b) of men, e.g., 1 Sam. 29:4; Ps. 38:20; 71:13; four in Ps. 109; (a) of "Satan the Devil, some seventeen or eighteen times in the OT; in Zech. 1, where the human receives its interpretation, to be (his) adversary," RV (see marg.: KJV, "TO RESIST HIM").

In the New Testament, the word is always of "Satan," the adversary (a) of God and Christ, e.g. Matt. 4:10; 12:26; Mark 1:13, 3:23; 26;

14 | THE OLD AND NEW TESTAMENT

4:15; Luke4:8) in some messages); 11:18; 22:3, John 13:27; (b) of His people., e.g. Luke 22:31;Acts:5:3; Rom:20; 1 Cor.5:5; 2Cor.2:11;; 11:14; 12:7; 1Thess.2:181 Tim.1:20:9; 5;15; Rev.2:9 13 (twice), 24;3:9; (s) of mankind, Luke 13:16; Acts26:18;2 . Thess. 2:9; Rev.12:9; 20:7. His doom sealed at the cross is foretold in its stages in Luke 10:18; Rev. 20:2, 10. Believers are assured of victory over him, Rom. 16:20. The application was given to Peter by the Lord AS A "Satan-man on the occasion when he endeavoured to dissuade Him from death, Matt. 16:23; Mark8:33.

Satan is not simply the personification of evil influences in the heart, for he tempted Christ, in whose heart no evil thought could ever arise (John 14:30; 2 Cor. 5:21; Heb. 4:15); moreover, his personality is asserted in both the OT and the NT, and especially in the latter; whereas if the OT language were intended to be figurative, the NT would have made this event.

SATISFY: OLD TESTAMENT

SABA: To be satisfied, sated, surfeited." Expresses the idea of "being filled, stated Exod. 16:8; often about eating, Jeremiah 50:19; Saba sometimes expresses "being surfeited with" Prov. 25:16; Isa. 1:11. Saba indicates God's satisfying, supplying man with his material needs (Psalm 103:5). However, even when God "fed them to the full," Israel was not satisfied and went after strange gods. Jer.5:7.

CHARTAZO: NEW TESTAMENT

THE OLD AND NEW TESTAMENT | 15

- To be filled or satisfied with food is translated as "satisfy" in Mark 8:4; KJV (RV, "to fill").

EMPIPLEMI:

To fill up, fill full, "satisfy" is used metaphorically in Rom. 15:24, RV, "I shall have been satisfied" KJV, I be filled"). Save or saving- The Old Testament.

SOZO: NEW TESTAMENT

In Hebrew, this word set 'wholeness' (soteria) "to be made whole" (sozo), might at least function as a corrective for one-sided rendering of "salvation," "salvation" "to be saved", and "Saviour"

"A VERB, TO SAVE," IS USED WITH THE NOUN "SORTERIA" (Mythology). An Ancient Greek word for the goddess or spirit of safety, salvation, deliverance, and perseverance from harm. It was also an epithet of the goddess Persephone, meaning deliverance and safety.

"Salvation" (a) of material and temporal deliverance from danger, suffering, etc., e.g., Matt. 8:25; Mark 13:20; Luke 23:35; John 12:27; 1 TIM. 2:15; 2 Tim. 4:18 KJV) "PRESERVE"); Jude 5; FROM SICKNESS, Matt. 9:22, "made" ………whole" Saved; Mark 5:34; Luke 8:48; Jas. 5:15 (b) of the spiritual and eternal salvation granted immediately by God to those who believe in the Lord Jesus Christ.

SAVIOR: SOTER "A SAVIOR, DELIVERER, PRESERVER, IS USED (a) Of God. Luke 1:47; 1 Tim. 1:1; 2:3; 4:10; in the sense of "preserver" since he gives "to all, life and breath and all things") Titus 1:3; 2:10; 3 4; Jude 25 (b) of Christ, Luke 2:11; John 4:42; Acts 5:31; 13:23; 9of Israel); Eph. 5:23; (the sustainer and preserver of the Church, His "body"); Phil. 3:20 (AT HIS RETURN TO RECEIVE THE CHURCH TO

HIMSELF); 2 Tim. 1:101 (concerning His incarnation, "the days of His flesh"); Titus 1:4 little

Share in the context, with God the Father); 2:3; RV, "our great God and Saviour Jesus Christ.

Continue in The Believers Code that man should see fit, living and acting in the ways and will of God.

- The Code of Conduct:

- The Code of Tolerance:

- The Code of Patience:

- The code of honesty:

- The Code of Humiliation:

- The Code of Perseverance:

- The code of Resilience

- The code of Overcoming

- The Code of Virtue:

- The Code of Integrity

- The Code of Love

- The Code of Forgiveness

- The Code of Christian Attire

- The Code of Consecration

The Code of Conduct is the way we are from the inner man and the way we are on the outer man, the bible says, and be not conformed to this world, but be ye transformed by the renewing of your mind, that ye may prove what is good and acceptable, and perfect will of God. Rom. 12:2 (KJV) Serve God with Spiritual gifts: vs 3, For I say, through the grace given unto me, to every man that is among you, not to think of himself more highly than he ought to think, but to think soberly, as God has dealt to every man the measure of faith.

Looking at the KJV, I therefore beseech you, brethren, by the mercies of God, that ye present your bodies a living sacrifice, holy, acceptable unto God, which is your reasonable service.

When we accept Jesus as our Lord and saviour, remember we did confess with our mouth and believe with our heart, Rom . 10.9 NKJV THAT IF YOU CONFESS WITH YOUR MOUTH THE LORD JESUS AND BELIEVE IN YOUR HEART that God has raised Him from the dead, you will be saved. This is what we did by our faith. God's Gift of "SALVATION" "SIN AND JUDGMENT" "MEET GRACE & MERCY".

Have you ever taken something that did not belong to you, told lies, or envied someone's possessions? What about hating another person or harbouring a lustful heart? When we are honest, EACH OF US WILL ADMIT TO DOING WRONG THINGS. Our wrong motives and actions condemn us as sinners who have missed the mark of God's holiness. Because of sin, each of us is justly sentenced to eternal separation from God. In this place of need, God invites us to come to Him and receive His gift of Salvation. Eph. 2:8-9 For by" GRACE" you have "FAITH" "BY GRACE YOU HAVE BEEN SAVED THROUGH FAITH, AND NOT OF YOURSELVES; IT IS THE GIFT OF GOD, NOT OF WORKS, LEST ANYONE SHOULD BOAST" 2 Cor. 5:21 "FOR HE MADE HIM

WHO KNEW NO SIN TO BE SIN FOR US, THAT WE MIGHT BECOME THE RIGHTEOUSNESS OF GOD IN HIM.

4. INTRODUCTION TO CHRISTIAN LIFE

Galatians 5:22-25 – The fruit of the Spirit is love, joy, peace, patience, kindness, goodness, faith, gentleness, self-control. Against such things24 And those who belong to Christ Jesus have crucified the flesh, with its passions and desires.

The apostle Paul lists nine things the Spirit of God produces for our well-being.

- If we live by the Spirit, we must also walk in the Spirit • The fruit (singular) is the by-product of Christ's control of our lives.

- They come to us through His will and with His help. • To have them, we must know Him, love Him, remember Him, and imitate Him.

- Paul's introduction of the word fruit is filled with meaning. While we might have expected him to say, "The works of the Spirit are," Paul needed to use a fresh term. He had used "works" enough throughout this letter.

- Besides, "works" (plural) indicates many activities people must do.

- "Fruit," however, is singular, indicating that all the fruits exist as a single

Unit (like a bunch of grapes rather than many different pieces of fruit) and that all are important to all believers; (unlike "gifts") that are dispensed differently to different people. So, Paul conveyed the meaning of a full harvest of virtues.

INTRODUCTION TO CHRISTIAN LIFE | 19

- Also, "fruit" is a by-product; it takes time to grow and requires care and cultivation. The Spirit produces the fruit; our job is to live harmoniously with the Spirit.

- The fruit of the Spirit separates Christians from a godless, evil world, reveals a power within them, and helps them become more Christ-like in their daily lives.

- The nine are easily divided into three categories: • THE FIRST THREE ARE INWARD AND COME FROM GOD. • Love

- Joy

- Peace

FRUIT OF THE SPIRIT: "The Fruit of the Spirit" 2. THE SECOND THREE CONCERN EACH CHRISTIAN'S RELATIONSHIPS WITH OTHERS:

- Patience

- Kindness

- Goodness

- THE FINAL THREE ARE MORE GENERAL TRAITS IN A CHRISTIAN'S LIFE.

- Faith

- Gentleness

- Self-control

INWARD FRUIT THAT COMES FROM GOD

- LOVE (agape)

- Love is shown by Jesus, whose love is self-sacrificing and unchanging, and as demonstrated by God, who sent his Son for sinners.

- Romans 5:8 – "But God proves His love for us in that while we were yet sinners Christ died for us!"

- Love forms the foundation for all the other fruits listed. Love seeks the best good of the one to whom it is directed. "Agape" love.

- Elsewhere, Paul breaks love itself down into various components (see 1

Corinthians 13), so "love" bears little resemblance to the emotional meaning so often given to the word.

JOY (chara)

- An inner rejoicing that abides despite outer circumstances. • This characteristic has little to do with happiness and can exist in times of unhappiness.

- It is a deep and nourishing satisfaction that continues even when a situation seems empty and unsatisfying.

- The relationship with God through Christ remains even in the deserts and valleys of living.

- PEACE (eirene)

- An inner quietness and trust in God's sovereignty and justice, even in adverse circumstances.

- This is a profound agreement with the truth that God, not we, remains in charge of the universe.

INWARD FRUIT THAT COMES FROM EACH CHRISTIAN'S RELATIONSHIPS WITH OTHERS.

FRUIT OF THE SPIRIT:

- "The Fruit of the Spirit"

- PATIENCE/LONGSUFFERING (makrothumia)

- Patiently putting up with people who continually irritate us. 2. The Holy Spirit's work helps us to increase our endurance.
  - KINDNESS (chrestotes)

- Acting charitably and benevolently toward others, as God did toward us. 2. Kindness takes the initiative in responding to other people's needs.

- GOODNESS (agathosune)

- Reaching out to do good to others, even if they don't deserve it.

- Goodness does not react to evil but absorbs the offence and responds with Positive action.

THE FINAL THREE ARE MORE GENERAL TRAITS IN A CHRISTIAN'S LIFE

- FAITHFULNESS (pistis)

- Faithfulness

- Reliable

- Trustworthy

- The Christian will be a faithful individual, an individual faithful to his word and promises; an individual.
-

Do you know whom you can trust or confide in?

- GENTLENESS (pratues)

- Humble, considerate of others,

submissive to God and his Word.

- Even when anger is the appropriate response, as when Jesus cleared the temple, gentleness keeps the expression of anger headed in the right direction

- Gentleness applies even force. C. SELF-CONTROL (egkrateia) • Mastery over sinful human desires and their lack of restraint. Ironically, our sinful desires, which promise self-fulfillment and power, inevitably lead us to slavery.

- When we surrender to God's will, we initially feel as though we have lost control, but He leads us to exercise self-control that would be impossible for us to achieve in our strength.

CONCLUSION:

- The Spirit produces these character traits found in Christ's nature.

- They are the by-products of Christ's

control; we can't obtain them by trying to get them without his help.

FRUIT OF THE SPIRIT: "The Fruit of the Spirit"

- If we want the fruit of the Spirit to grow in us, we must align our lives to his.

John 15:4-5 – Remain in Me, and I in you. Just as a branch is unable to bear fruit unless it remains on the vine, it produces fruit, so neither can you.

- To understand the fruit of the Spirit, we must see ourselves not as individual trees but as an entire garden under the cultivation of God's Spirit.

INTRODUCTION TO CHRISTIAN LIFE | 23

- His purpose involves producing not simply a single kind of fruit but all the fruit, each becoming ripe as needed.

- No one person can perfectly exemplify all the fruit all the time. c. We are all needed to produce God's harvest of virtue. d. We must not be discouraged if our love or patience is not perfect. e. Don't let your lack of fruitfulness in some areas destroy what God is trying to do for you today.

- A wonderful salvation awaits you with your obedience to Christ. B. GOD'S PLAN FOR MAN'S SALVATION

- "I am the vine; you are the branches. The one!

Unless you remain in Me, who remains in Me, and I in him, you can do nothing without Me.

- We must know him.

- We must love him.

- We must remember him.

- We must imitate him.

Jesus said in Jn. 15:1-5, "Every branch in me that does not bear fruit he (God) takes away, and every branch that does bear fruit he prunes, that it may bear more fruit. I am the vine; you are the branches. If you remain in me and I in you, you will bear much fruit; apart from me, you can do nothing.

There is a parable that Jesus tells of 10 virgins. Some ran out of oil, and some did not. Those who did not were unable to enter heaven. The question is, where are all the virgins in the parable of the Christian? Could it be that some of the Christians ran out of the Holy Spirit, since oil represents the Holy Spirit in the Bible, and so they did not get to enter heaven? Could some have been what Jesus spoke of, branches that did not bear fruit anymore, and so they were taken away? Either way, it is crucial that a Christian bears fruit and continues to bear fruit throughout their whole life.

Jesus said in Jn. 15:1-5, "Every branch in me that does not bear fruit he (God) takes away, and every branch that does bear fruit he prunes, that it may bear more fruit. I am the vine; you are the branches. If you remain in me and I in you, you will bear much fruit; apart from me you can do nothing."

Jesus tells a parable about 10 virgins. Some ran out of oil, and some did not. The ones who did not could not enter heaven. The question is, where are all the virgins in the parable?

Christian? Could it be that some of the Christians ran out of the Holy Spirit, since oil represents the Holy Spirit in the Bible, and so they did not get to enter heaven? Could some have been what Jesus spoke of, branches that did not bear fruit anymore, and so they were taken away? Either way, it is crucial that a Christian bears fruit and continues to bear fruit throughout their whole life.

5. A TREE RECOGNIZED BY ITS FRUIT

Matthew 7:15-23; Matt. 12:33-37 KJV

33 Either makes the tree good, and his fruit good; or else makes the tree corrupt, and his fruit corrupt: for the tree is known by his fruit. 34 O generation of vipers, how can ye, being evil, speak good things? For out of the abundance of the heart the mouth speaketh. 35 A good man out of the good treasure of the heart bringeth good things, and an evil man out of the evil treasure bringeth evil things. 36 But I say unto you, that every idle word that men shall speak, they shall give account thereof in the Day of Judgment. 37 For by thy words thou shalt be justified, and by thy words thou shalt be condemned.

The Human Problem: We humans often

face challenges. When we have problems, we often create solutions that are bigger problems in disguise. After that, we find out that we have actually upgraded the problems.

Then, we create more problems to solve the existing ones, and hope that the problems we create (solutions) do not lead to too many problems (side effects).

At first, we got tired of travelling with animals. We thought they were the problem, so we created cars. Now, cars are the problem. We need to solve that problem, mainly because we require fresh air.

We grew tired of fighting long, drawn-out wars. We thought weapons were the problem, so we developed deadly weapons to intimidate our enemies into making peace. Now, weapons are the problem.

We also wanted to be happier and thought healthy foods were the problem. We wanted something faster and sweeter, so we created soda and processed sugars. Now, junk food is the problem.

We got tired of stressing ourselves. Thinking our lifestyle was the problem, we created a life that kept us sedentary. Now, the lifestyle is the problem. We want to exercise.

We also thought that we needed more knowledge; we believed ignorance was the problem. Then, laziness, inactivity, apathy, and overintellectualization set in, and we realized that excessive knowledge was the new problem.

We thought we needed faster ways to share our lives and thoughts. We thought the problem was the communication platform, so we created social media. We then realized that it destroys communication and erodes people's sanity.

And then we found the real problem—the problem that had wrecked all previous solutions, the most significant problem. We discovered that the problem is reading this right now: YOU! You are the problem because you are a living human.

We also need to solve this problem. Hopefully, after solving this problem, we'll have no more problems. What is a very 'human' problem? Humans are quicker to follow the world's behaviour and actions, engaging in worldly things, staying within their comfort zone, and speaking of nothing substantial about God. Humans tend to stick to the norm, what they know or see in life. The bible says, "Seek ye first the kingdom of God and all these things shall be added unto thee."

- What are the fundamental problems with human beings?

Copycatting plays a significant role in human lives, so to speak! They seem to follow the people and their

Ways, and not so easily following Jesus.

- What is the main problem of a human

being? They don't recognize that we as humans were created by the

one and only creator, who is God himself; The

Father, the Son, and the Holy Ghost; they are one.

Divinity.

- What makes a problem a human problem? Self- they rely on self and man-made remedies, but in John 14:6

tell us; no man cometh unto the Father, but through me, Jesus!

The root of every human problem is a deep-seated, basic selfishness in each of us. We are motivated by what is best for us, even if it's buried deep beneath all the fluff we tell ourselves. Do you feed the hungry? How much satisfaction do you take from this act? Do you volunteer at homeless shelters? What's it like when you receive praise from others for your sacrifice?

We all derive something from every "selfless" act we do that is positive for us. If we don't, we don't continue to do that exercise. This doesn't make us evil. It has a sense of balance. We don't solve our problems all by ourselves. All humans are convinced since birth that they are a physical body-COMPLEX in a world perceived only through this COMPLEX; and therefore, remain ignorant of their existential reality and go on adding additional false "IDENTITY" OF "RELIGION", cast, greed, gender, and colour.

"This is the fundamental problem! This fundamental flaw can only be eliminated by liberating the human mind from this condition.

God has given us free will to choose! As the effects of sin corrupt humans, prevenient grace allows persons to engage their God given free will to choose the salvation offered by God in Jesus Christ or to reject that salvific offer.

As the effects of sin corrupt humans, prevenient grace allows persons to engage their God-given free will to choose the salvation offered by God in Jesus Christ or to reject that salvific offer.

1 COR. 5:17 KJV Therefore, if any man is in Christ Jesus, he is a new creature; old things have passed away; all things have become new. Free will in theology is a central aspect of the broader debate. Religions vary greatly in their response to the standard argument against free will. They thus might appeal to any number of responses to the paradox of free will, the claim that omniscience and free will are incompatible.

Many Christian churches and denominations have different views on free will. While it's easy to become confused about how God's control and our free will interact, we can trust the Word of God and know that what He has told us in the Bible is true. These Bible verses about free will demonstrate that we can choose to have faith in God, be secure in our eternal life in heaven, or choose to turn away from God and live apart from Him. Use these

Scriptures to help you make wise choices!

1 Corinthians 10:13 (NIV)

"No temptation has overtaken you except what is common to mankind. And God is faithful; he will not let you be tempted beyond what you can bear. But when you are tempted, he will also provide a way out so that you can endure it."

6. WARNING FROM ISRAEL

- For I do not want to be ignorant, brothers and sisters, that our ancestors were all under the cloud and passed through the sea.

- They were all baptized into Moses in the cloud and the sea.

- - They all ate the same spiritual food.

- They drank the same spiritual drink, from the spiritual rock that accompanied them, and that rock was Christ.

- Nevertheless, God was not pleased with most of them; their bodies were scattered in the wilderness.

- These were examples to keep us from setting our hearts on evil things as they did.

- Do not be idolaters, as some were; as it is written: "The people sat down to eat and drink and got up to indulge in revelry."

- • We should not commit sexual immorality, as some of them did, and in one day, twenty-three thousand of them died.

- • We should not test Christ, as some of them did, and were killed by snakes.

- And do not grumble, as some of them did—and were killed by the destroying angel.

- These things happened to them as examples and were written down as warnings for us, on whom the culmination of the ages has come.

- So, if you think you are standing firm, be careful that you don't fall!

- No temptation has overtaken you except what is common to mankind. And God is faithful; he will not let you be tempted beyond what you can bear. But when you are tempted, he will also provide a way out so that you can endure it. (1 Cor. 10:1-13) NIV

1. God says, Call upon me on the day of trouble, and I will give you rest; At that time, Jesus went on the Sabbath day through the corn, and his disciples were hungry, and began to pluck the ears of corn, and to eat.

2. But when the Pharisees saw it, they said unto him, Behold, thy disciples do that which is not lawful to do upon the Sabbath day.

3. But he said unto them, Have ye not read what David did? When he was hungry, and those with him were hungry. How he entered into the house of God, and did eat the showbread, which was not lawful for him to eat, neither for them which were with him, but only for the priests?

4. Or have ye not read in the law, how on the Sabbath days the priests in the temple profane the Sabbath, and are blameless?

5. But I say unto you that this place is one

greater than the temple.

6. But if ye had known what this meaneth, I will have mercy, and not sacrifice, ye would not have condemned the guiltless.

7. For the Son of man is Lord even on the Sabbath day. (Matt.12:1-8) NIV

7. JESUS HEALS ON THE SABBATH

Matthew 12 1-37 KJV

1. At that time, Jesus went on the Sabbath day through the corn; and his disciples were hungry, and began to pluck the ears of corn and to eat.

² But when the Pharisees saw it, they said unto him, Behold, thy disciples do that which is not lawful to do upon the sabbath day.

³ But he said unto them, Have ye not read what David did, when he was an hungred, and they that were with him?

⁴ How he entered into the house of God, and did eat the shewbread, which was not lawful for him to eat, neither for

them which were with him, but only for the priests?

⁵ Or have ye not read in the law, how that on the sabbath days the priests in the temple profane the sabbath, and are blameless?

⁶ But I say unto you, That in this place is one greater than the temple.

⁷ But if ye had known what this meaneth, I will have mercy, and not sacrifice, ye would not have condemned the guiltless.

⁸ For the Son of man is Lord even of the sabbath day.

⁹ And when he was departed thence, he went into their synagogue:

¹⁰ And, behold, there was a man whose hand was withered. And they asked him, saying, 'Is it lawful to heal on the Sabbath days?' that they might accuse him.

¹¹ And he said unto them, What man shall there be among you, that shall have one sheep, and if it fall into a pit on the sabbath day, will he not lay hold on it, and lift it out?

¹² How much then is a man better than a sheep? Wherefore it is lawful to do well on the sabbath days.

¹³ Then saith he to the man, Stretch forth thine hand. And he stretched it forth; and it was restored whole, like as the other.

¹⁴ Then the Pharisees went out and held a council against him, how they might destroy him.

¹⁵ But when Jesus knew it, he withdrew himself from thence: and great multitudes followed him, and he healed them all;

¹⁶ And charged them that they should not make him known:

¹⁷ That it might be fulfilled which was spoken by Esaias the prophet, saying,

¹⁸ Behold my servant, whom I have chosen; my beloved, in whom my soul is well pleased: I will put my spirit upon him, and he shall shew judgment to the Gentiles.

¹⁹ He shall not strive, nor cry; neither shall any man hear his voice in the streets.

²⁰ A bruised reed shall he not break, and smoking flax shall he not quench, till he send forth judgment unto victory.

²¹ And in his name shall the Gentiles trust.

²² Then was brought unto him one possessed with a devil, blind, and dumb: and he healed him, insomuch that the blind and dumb both spake and saw.

²³ And all the people were amazed, and said, Is not this the son of David?

²⁴ But when the Pharisees heard it, they said, This fellow doth not cast out devils, but by Beelzebub the prince of the devils.

²⁵ And Jesus knew their thoughts, and said unto them, Every kingdom divided against itself is brought to desolation; and every city or house divided against itself shall not stand:

²⁶ And if Satan cast out Satan, he is divided against himself; how then shall his kingdom stand?

²⁷ And if I by Beelzebub cast out devils, by whom do your children cast them out? Therefore, they shall be your judges.

²⁸ But if I cast out devils by the Spirit of God, then the kingdom of God is come unto you.

²⁹ Or else how can one enter into a strong man's house, and spoil his goods, except he first bind the strong man? And

then he will spoil his house.

³⁰ He that is not with me is against me; and he that gathereth not with me scattereth abroad.

³¹ Wherefore I say unto you, All manner of sin and blasphemy shall be forgiven unto men: but the blasphemy against the Holy Ghost shall not be forgiven unto men.

³² And whosoever speaketh a word against the Son of man, it shall be forgiven him: but whosoever speaketh against the Holy Ghost, it shall not be forgiven him, neither in this world, neither in the world to come.

³³ Either make the tree good, and his fruit good; or else make the tree corrupt, and his fruit corrupt: for the tree is known by his fruit.

³⁴ O generation of vipers, how can ye, being evil, speak good things? for out of

the abundance of the heart the mouth speaketh.

³⁵ A good man out of the good treasure of the heart bringeth forth good things: and an evil man out of the evil treasure bringeth forth evil things.

³⁶ But I say unto you, That every idle word that men shall speak, they shall give account thereof in the day of judgment.

³⁷ For by thy words thou shalt be justified, and by thy words thou shalt be condemned.

A good man out of the good treasure of the heart brings forth good things, and an evil man out of the evil treasure brings forth evil things. But I say unto you, that every idle word that men shall speak, they shall give account thereof in the Day of Judgment. For by thy words thou shalt be justified, and by thy words thou shalt be condemned.

Paul had told the Philippians that Jesus was his life, joy, and one consuming passion. "For to me, to live is Christ, and to die is gain" (Philippians 1:21) . Paul wanted Jesus to be exalted in his body in every way,"Whether by life or by death" (v.20). And death was certainly a possibility if his accusers had their way in court or an ambush on some deserted road.

The thought of Martyrdom didn't depress Paul; he got downright homesick at the prospect of being in heaven with Jesus, unshackled and free. Dying would really be a "gain" for Paul. And that's the essence of his dilemma. But if I am to live on in the flesh, this will mean fruitful labour for me, and I do not know which to choose.

But I am hard-pressed from both directions, wanting to depart and be in Christ, for that is much better; yet, remaining in the flesh is more necessary for your sake. (v. 22—24) The Apostle's desire to join Jesus in heaven and yet remain with the Philippians on earth leaves him between a rock and a hard place. (v. 22) As in all dilemmas, both sides have benefits and liabilities. Let's take a brief look at some of these for Paul.

Philippians' Spiritual Challenges

Having committed himself to remain, Paul immediately issues a challenge to ensure the Philippians' "progress and joy in the faith"

Only conduct yourselves in a manner worthy of the gospel of Christ; so that whether I come and see or remain absent, I may hear of you that you are standing firm in one spirit, with one mind striving together for the faith of the gospel; in so way by alarmed by your opponents-which is a sign of destruction for them, but of salvation for you, and that too, from GOD. For you it has been granted for Christ's sake, not only to believe in Him, but also to suffer for His sake, experiencing the same Conflict which you saw in me, and now here to be in me.

1. (27—30)

What did Paul mean by Conduct? To be worthy of the gospel of Christ, let us examine both the positive and negative aspects of this challenge.

Positive: The Philippians were told to stand firm in one spirit with one mind (vs. 27b). In two aspects, first, Paul wanted them to be united and harmonious. And second, before others, they are to exhibit solidarity and courage in striving for the gospel. In Greek, the word for striving is an athletic, blood, sweat, and tears kind of term. The Philippians have seen Paul fight the good fight of faith by the sweat of his brow; now he exhorts them to do the same.

Negative: Paul tells them not to be "alarmed by their opponents." The battle term pictures a horse shying away from the battlefield. The Philippians aren't to go out looking for trouble, but there is no reason to be shy or hesitant when conflicts flare up. And the apostle gives them several reasons why.

They are not alone (v.27). They are to strive together for the gospel. It's fighting to face opposition alone, but there is comfort in having others on your side, who are also by your side.

Paul assures them that, ultimately, the victory is theirs (v. 28). The presence of opposition, Paul assures them, demonstrates that they are on the right path in their Active gospel witness. It is a token of salvation to them, as it is a token of perdition for their opponents: "they will lose…. you will win" (GNB). God is the gospel's author: those who defend it may expect deliverance from and victory over him as surely as those who resist it may expect to incur his judgment. A similar thought is given fuller expression in 2 Thessalonians 1:5-10. Read!

The Philippians shouldn't be alarmed by their opponents because God has granted that His followers should suffer for His sake (Philippians 1:29). This is a painful but helpful reminder. Don't let opposition and suffering catch you off guard; prepare for them by expecting them.

Paul helps calm the Philippians' fear by

reminding them that he has faced the same conflict they face (Phil. 2:30). Hope and encouragement often come from knowing that someone else has already been through what you're currently experiencing.

Our Response

Making the right decisions amid a dilemma is tough. It compels us to reassess our priorities and reevaluate the significance of Christ in our lives.

Have you recently faced a dilemma? Have you been torn between two directions by rock-and-hard-place decisions?

Choosing the best solutions won't be easy. So put on your bifocals if you need them; muster all the wisdom you can from experience; and don't forget to keep your commitment to Christ as strong, black, and defined as Paul's: "For to me, to live in Christ, to die is gain." (v.21) KJV.

8. THE HIDDEN SECRET OF A HAPPY LIFE

Code of Conduct:

Philippians 2:1-11

Of all the Christ-like attitudes that people exhibit in our world, rarely do any of them grab our hearts and minds like unselfishness, whether it is the selfless work of a well-known Mother Teresa or an unknown man in the water. As disasters go, this one was terrible, but not unique, certainly not among the worst roster of U.S. air crashes. There was, of course, the unusual element of the bridge, and the plane clipped it at a moment of high traffic, one routine thus intersecting another and disrupting both.

Additionally, the event's location played a role. The disaster happens, the plane crashes, and there was nothing very special in this, except death, which, while always special, does not necessarily bring millions to tears or attention. Why, then, the shock here? The person most responsible for the disaster's emotional impact is the one known at first simply as "the man in the water." He was seen clinging to the tail section of the airplane with five other survivors. Usher and Windsor described this man.

(A park police helicopter team) appearing alert and in control. Every time they lowered a lifeline and a flotation ring to him, he passed them to another passenger. In a mass casualty, you'll find people like Windsor. "But I've never seen one with that commitment." When the helicopter came back for him, the man had gone under. His selflessness was one reason the story held national attention.

Analyzing Unselfishness

We all have our definitions to describe it, but words cannot explain the meaning and forcefulness of that man's ultimate act of self-sacrifice in the icy waters of the Potomac.

At some moment in the water, he must have realized that he would not live if he continued to hand over the rope and ring to others. He had to know it, no matter how gradual the effect of the cold. In his judgment, he had no choice. When the helicopter took off with what was to be the last survivor, he watched everything in the world move away from him, and he deliberately let it happen.

That costly sacrifice powerfully portrays another. Two thousand years ago, the Son of God became flesh and dwelt among us. He came to pay the penalty for our sins, knowing it would cost Him His life. In his judgment, however, He had no choice.

When his betrayer took off and the disciple fled, he watched everything moving away from him. And he deliberately let it happen. That's unselfishness; that's Christ's likeness in one word.

Examining Christ's likeness

Christ's likeness is also Paul's primary concern in our lesson today. He wants LYDIA, the Roman jailer, and the rest of the believers in Philippi to exemplify this same selfless attitude—an attitude essential to the church's unity, THEN AND NOW!

What Is Needed?

In the first two verses, Paul encourages selflessness expressed in a spirit of harmony. If there is any encouragement in Christ, if there is any consolation of love, if there is any fellowship of the Spirit, if any affection and compassion, make my joy complete by being of the same mind. Maintaining the same love, united in spirit, intent on one purpose. (Phil. 2:1-2) NIV

To better understand the implication of Paul's foretold plea, reread verse 1 and change each "if there is" to "since there foretold this, you will see that Paul is affirming these qualities in the Philippians, not questioning them. Then note how these four assertions link with the four requests in verse two.

- Since there is encouragement in Christ, agree.

- Since there is consolation in love, maintain that same love.

- Since there is fellowship of the Spirit, be united in spirit.

- Since there is affection and compassion, be intent on one purpose.

By encouraging the Philippians to be "of the same mind," Is Paul saying there is no room for individuality and disagreement? Not at all. Is it unity that we should all think, dress, and act the same, like the Church? He is not pleading for infirmity. And there is a big difference. Unity comes from within; it's the result of an inner attitude. Uniformity, conversely, comes from without, the forced product of external pressure. In his commentary on Philippians, Harry

Ironside provides insight into achieving unity amidst diversity.

Christians will never agree on all points. We are so influenced mainly by habits, the environment, education, and the measure of intellectual and spiritual apprehension we have attained, that it is Impossible.

The word "if" is the translation of a conditional particle referring to a fulfilled condition.

One could translate 'since' or given the fact. The four things mentioned in this verse are not hypothetical. They are facts. Kenneth S. Wuest, Wuest's Word Studies from the Greek New Testament (1973); reprint, Grand Rapids, Mich.: William B. Eerdmans Publishing Co. (1979), vol. p. 56.

It is a responsibility to find several people who look at everything from the same standpoint. How then can one be of one mind? The apostle explains it elsewhere when he says, "I think also that I have the mind of Christ." "The mind of Christ " is the lowly mind, and we shall walk together in love, considering one another and seeking to be helpers of one another's faith rather than challenging each other's convictions.

The lowly mind of Christ is a selfless one. That's what is needed if there is to be any hope of unity.

9. HOW IS IT ACCOMPLISHED

Practical advice on integrating a Christ-like attitude into every aspect of life is also needed if unity is ever to become more than just a nice idea. And Paul provides this kind of prudent counsel in verses 3-4.NIV

Do nothing from selfishness or empty conceit, but with humility of mind, let each of you regard one another as more important than yourself; do not merely look out for your interest but also for the interest of others.

The three practical tips Paul mentions are :

(1) Never let selfishness or conceit be your motive;

(2) regard others as more important than

yourself;

(3) Don't limit your attention to your interests, including others. Self-forgetfulness is what Paul is advocating, not self-hate. As Christians, when we pursue the gold of exalting Christ and putting others before ourselves, we tend to forget all the self-serving, petty differences that usually separate us.

So, instead of waiting for external reasons to draw us together, Paul would have us initiate a lasting unity through a Christ-like attitude. And who is there to learn this from than Christ Himself?

CHRIST'S LIFE – BEFORE & AFTER

In this next section of his letter, Paul reveals Christ's humble attitude by showing us his life before, during, and after He came to earth.

BEFORE HIS INCARNATION

To highlight Jesus' lowliness of mind, Paul first reveals the height of glory the preexistent Saviour enjoys in heaven.

Having this attitude in yourself was also in Christ Jesus; although He existed in the form of God, He did not regard equality with God as something to be grasped. (V:5-6)

According to commentator Alfred Plummer, "In the form of God" means 'possessing the Divine attributes." As the second member of the Godhead, Jesus is coexistent, coeternal, and coequal with God. His life didn't begin in Mary's womb. The only thing that began within Mary was the manifestation of the Son of God. For the first time, God became flesh and blood.

However, Jesus didn't regard His exalted position as something to be grasped. Nothing within Him tempted Him to snatch or seize all the benefits of His role as absolute Sovereign. Why? Because of His lowliness of mind, His unselfish attitude. Jesus willingly released it all for humanity in absolute perfection and complete control.

Encompassed by an angelic host who praised and adored Him, the Saviour unselfishly came to those who cursed and crucified Him. Surrounded by the Father's presence and fellowship, He unhesitatingly gave it all up for a lonely path of obedience to the cross.

Consider the steps Jesus took downward to share our humanity and die for our sins.

- He emptied Himself.

- He took the form of a bond servant.

- He humbled himself by becoming obedient unto death

- He accepted the most humiliating type of death: Crucifixion.

To accomplish our salvation on a cross, Jesus first had to empty Himself. This does not mean that He gave up His deity; rather, it signifies that Christ set aside the independent use of His Divine attributes and submitted to the Father's will.

SINCE HIS DEPARTURE:

The Father's will mandated that Jesus descend into the lowest depths of suffering and hell for our sins. But once our debt was paid, God again exalted His Son to the highest glory and honour.

Therefore, also God highly exalted Him, and bestowed on Him the name which is above every name, that at the name of "JESUS" EVERY KNEE SHOULD BOW, OF THOSE WHO ARE IN HEAVEN, AND ON EARTH, AND UNDER THE EARTH, AND THAT EVERY TONGUE SHOULD CONFESS THAT JESUS CHRIST IS LORD, TO THE GLORY OF GOD THE FATHER. (Phil. 2:9-11). NASB

God not only exalted Jesus to a higher position but also bestowed on Him the name of highest significance. He who willingly bowed to the Father's will in coming is now the recipient of all knees bowing to Him. Those in heaven will bow, which means the angelic host and all the believers who have died before us. Those on earth will bow, which includes everyone from the most bitter skeptic to the most sincere followers. And those who are under the earth will bow, which refers to the unsaved who have died, the demonic host, and even Satan himself.

10. REFLECTIONS

"Let us reflect on some of the important attributes of a believer."

The code of honour; who to honour? Those above us, who have the authority to guide, teach, etc., our leaders, parents, and why we must honour them? They are the ones God has placed in our lives to show and uplift us, teaching us new things through their knowledge and the experiences that led them to where they are. Parents!

The bible says; Honour thy mother and thy father, that your days may be long upon the land. Deuteronomy 5:16 KJV "Honour thy father and thy mother, as the Lord thy God hath commanded thee; that thy days may be prolonged, and that it may go well with thee, in the which the Lord giveth thee."

The code of "Christians' Attire should be, and how they must present themselves!

A Christian must dress in a manner that reveals/manifests God to the world and in a manner that does not make a brother or a sister sin.

What are your thoughts after reading this?

_____

_____

_____

_____

_____

What is the tolerance code, and how have you addressed it?

_____

_____

_____

The code of patients, and how you have seen yourself at this stage in your walk?

What is the code of humility and/or humiliation by others or someone in the Church?

The code of perseverance in life's trials and tribulations—how have you dealt with this?

_____

_____

_____

_____

What did you have to endure through affliction?

_____

The code of being an overcomer, "They overcame by the blood of the lamb, and by the words of their testimony." (Rev. 12:11)KJV

How would you say you have overcome?

The code of resilience; (getting back up) how have you dwelled with this? And what inspired you to make that comeback?

The code of virtue: What is your experience of being the Proverbs 31 woman? As in the bible

The code of integrity from a Christian perspective is the quality of being honest and upholding strong moral principles. What is your view on integrity in the Christian way?

The Code of Love: What does God say about love in Scripture?

It is God's commandment! Jesus was speaking to the Pharisees in the Old Testament.

(Matt. 22:34-40) KJV

But they gathered together when the Pharisees heard that he had silenced the Sadducees. Saying, Master, which is the great commandment in the law?

Jesus said unto him, thou shalt love the Lord thy God with all thy heart, and with all thy soul, and with all thy mind.

This is the first and great commandment.

And the second is like unto it, Thou shalt love thy neighbour as thyself.

On these two commandments hang all the law and the prophets.

According to Paul, the Corinthians were so enthusiastic about flashy spiritual gifts, such as speaking in tongues, that they overlooked the greater importance of love, which undergirds all gifts. For Paul, God's love is joined with truth (1 Corinthians 13:6), KJV.

Love is an integral part of God's covenant with Israel: it is a human response to God's love and mercy. When Moses had descended from Mount Sinai a second time with the newly engraved tablet of commandment, he summarized what God requires of the Israelites: they are to 1) fear the Lord, 2) walk in all his ways, 3) love him, 4) serve the Lord, and 5) keep the commandments of the Lord. Deut. 10: 12-13). Every repetition of this summary by Moses prioritizes the commandment to love God (Deut. 11 1-22, Deut. 19:9, Deut. 30:16-20, Josh. 22:5). Love is intimately tied to obeying God.

Jesus continued the earlier covenant's emphasis on love of God, which includes obedience; "if you love me, you will keep my commandments"(for example in John 14:15-24). Jesus gives his disciples a "new" commandment, that you love one another, "how can loving one another be a new covenant, when love was a team in the earlier covenant? Jesus clarifies (after just having washed his Disciples' feet). "Just as I have loved you, you also should love one another. By this, everyone will know that you are my disciples. "If you have love for one another" (John 13:34-35).

Jesus's sacrificial love embodies the ultimate expression of love. Jesus laid down his life for others (John 3:16; Eph. 5:2 Jesus says! And walk in love, as Christ also hath loved us, and hath given himself for us an offering and a sacrifice to God for a sweet-smelling saviour. His new commandment is to love as Jesus loved (and as God has loved Israel, with Chesed). It is a Hebrew word in its original sense; it is used to describe kindness or love between people, the devotion of people towards God, and the love or mercy of God towards humanity. Such love is a sign to others of God's covenant.

11. THE FALL OF MAN: THE NATURE AND FINAL CONSEQUENCES OF SIN

The consequences of Adam's first sin may be considered under the following headings: depravity, guilt, and penalty.

Depravity

The meaning of Depravity: Man's want of original righteousness, holy affections towards God, and the corruption of his moral nature and his bias toward evil is called depravity. Its existence is attested by both Scripture and human experience. The teaching of Scripture that all men must be born again shows the universality of its existence.

From the positive standpoint, it does mean that every sinner is destitute of that love to God which is the fundamental requirement of the law (Deut. 6:4; Matt. 22:37)KJV that he is supremely given to a preference of himself to God (2 Tim. 3:2-4); that he have an aversion to God which on occasion becomes active enmity to him (Rom. 8:7); that is every faculty is disordered and corrupted (Eph. 4: 18); that he has no thought, feeling, or deed of which God can fully approved (Rom. 7:18); and that he has entered upon a line of constant progress in depravity from which he can in no wise turn away in his strength (Rom. 7:18). Depravity has infected the whole man—mind and will.

Depravity has produced a total spiritual inability in the sinner, in the sense that he cannot, by his own volition, change his character

and life to make them conform to the law of God, nor change his fundamental preference for self and sin to a supreme love for God. Yet he has some freedom left. He can, for instance, choose not to sin against the Holy Spirit, commit the lesser sin rather than the greater, resist certain forms of temptation altogether, do certain outwardly good acts, though with improper and unspiritual motives, and even seek God from entirely selfish motives.

Freedom of choice within these limits is not incompatible with complete bondage of the will to spiritual things. Inability consists not in the loss of any faculty of the soul, nor in the loss of free agency, for the sinner still determines his acts, nor in the mere disinclination to what is good, but in want of spiritual discernment, and therefore of proper affections.

He cannot of his free will regenerate himself, repent, or exercise saving faith. Yet to all who did receive him, to those who believe in his name, he gave the right to become children of God. (John 1:12) NIV But the grace and Spirit of God are ready to enable him to repent and believe unto salvation.

Guilt

The fact that guilt follows depravity does not mean it comes later. Both consequences came upon man simultaneously as a result of the fall. In a discussion of guilt, its meaning and the decrees of guilt must be considered.

The Meaning of Guilt—Guilt means the desert of punishment, or the obligation to satisfy God. God's holiness, as the Scriptures show, reacts against sin, and this is "the wrath of God" (Rom. 1:18). KJV But guilt is incurred only through self-chosen transgression, either on the part of humanity in Adam or on the part of the person.

Guilt comes from sin, of which we have had a part. Sin as

pollution is unlike God's character, but as guilt, it is an antagonism to his holy will. Both elements are ever-present in the conscience of the sinner. Guilt is also an objective result of sin, for every sin, of whatever nature, is an offence against God and subject to his wrath.

It must be confused with the subjective consciousness of it. It is primarily a relation to God, and secondarily a relation to conscience. In conscience, God's condemnation partially and prophetically manifests itself (1 John 3:20), ref. (read) A diminished sensitivity to moral discernment and feeling will mark the persistence and progress of sin.

The Degrees of Guilt: The scriptures recognize different degrees of guilt arising from various sins. The principle is recognized in the Old Testament in a variety of sacrifices required for different transgressions under the Mosaic law (Lev. 4-7)KJV It is also indicated in the variety of judgments in the New Testament (Luke 12:47) John 19:11; Rom. 2:6 Heb. 2:2f 10:28.)KJV The Roman Catholic has, however, built up an enormous distinction between venial and moral sins; venial sins are those which can be forgiven, and mortal sins are those which are willful and deliberate and involve death to the soul. Over this, we may note the two differences in guilt resulting from differences in sin.

There are at least four sets of contrasting sins.

Sin is in nature and personal transgression. Man is a sinner by nature and by act. There is a guilt of inborn sin and greater guilt when the sinful nature causes man to commit acts of personal transgression. The words of Christ, "the kingdom of heaven belongs to such as these" (Matt. 19:14) KJV, speak of the relative innocence of childhood, while his words to the Pharisees and the Scribes, "fill up then the measure of the guilt of your fathers" (Matt. 23:32-37) KJV, Refer to personal transgression added to inherited depravity.

58 | THE FALL OF MAN: THE NATURE AND FINAL CONSEQUENCES OF SIN

Sins of ignorance, and sins of knowledge. Here, guilt is determined according to the amount of information the individual possesses. The greater the degree of knowledge, the greater the guilt (Matt. 10:15; Luke 12:47; 23:34; Rom. 1:32; 2:13; 1 Tim. 1:13-16) KJV

Sins of weakness and sins of presumption. The strength of will involved here indicates the degree of guilt. The Psalmist prayed to be kept from presumptuous sins (Psalm 19:13) KJV, and Isaiah spoke of those who drag iniquity with the cords of falsehood, and sin as if with cart ropes" (Isaiah 5:18) KJV These are they who knowingly and determinately indulge in sin. On the other hand, Peter is determined to stand (Luke

22:31-34, 54-62). KJV; NIV It is interesting to note that there was no sacrifice for willful sinning (Num. 15:30; 10:26) KJV; NIV

Sin of incompleteness, and sin of complete hardheartedness. The degree to which the soul has hardened itself and become unreceptive to multiplied offers of the grace of God here determines the degree of guilt. A soul may turn from the love of truth and become utterly insensitive to the Spirit's promptings (1 Tim. 4:2; Heb. 6:4-6; 10:26; 2 Pet. 2:20-22; 1 John 2:19; 5:16) KJV; NIV.

PENALTY

While it is true that, to a certain extent, the natural consequences of sin are a part of the penalty of sin, we must remember that the full penalty is different. Depravity and guilt, as consequences of sin, rest upon mankind now, but the penalty awaits a future day.

The meaning of Penalty:

A penalty is pain or loss directly inflicted by the lawgiver in vindication of justice, outraged by the violation of law. This implies and includes the natural consequences of sin, but these by no means exhaust that penalty. In all penalties, there is a personal element, the holy wrath of the lawgiver, which is only partially expressed by the natural consequences. The penalty is not mainly aimed at reforming the offender.

There is a difference between discipline and punishment. Discipline proceeds from love and is intended to be corrective (Jer. 10:24; 2 Cor. 2:6-8; 1 Tim. 1:20; Heb. 12:6); SEE KJV; NIV but punishment proceeds from justice and is not intended to reform the offender. (Ezek. 28 22; 36:21; Rev. 16:5; 19:2). KJV; NIV Neither is it primarily intended as a deterrent and preventive, though this end is sometimes secured, for it is never right to punish an individual simply for the good of society, nor will punishment do good unless the person punished deserves punishment.

Punishment inflicted by law is not discipline nor remedy, but just retribution. It is not a means, but an end. A murderer is not corrected by being put to death; he is receiving a just retribution for his deed. Capital punishment is a divine mandate (Gen. 9:5), KJV. NIV; SEE REFERENCES

The Character of Penalty:

It takes only one word to state the penalty of sin, which is given in the Scripture: Death. It is a threefold death: physical and eternal.

Physical Death:

Physical death is the separation of the soul and body. It is represented in Scripture as part of the penalty for sin. This is the most natural meaning of Gen. 2:17; 3:19; Num. 16:29; 27:3 in the KJV and NIV. The prayer of Moses (Ps. 90:7-11) and the prayer of Hezekiah (Isaiah 3:8:17) in the KJV recognize the penal character of death.

The same thing is true in the New Testament (John 8:44; Rom. 4:24; 5:12-17; 8:3; 10f.; Gal 3:13; 1 Pet. 4:6). KJV; NIV For the

Christian, however, death is no longer a penalty, since Christ has endured death as the penalty of sins. (Ps. 17:15; 2 Cor. 5:8; Phil. 1:22-23; 1 Thess. 4:13). KJV; NIV For him the body sleeps, awaiting the glories of the presence of the Lord. Jesus.

Spiritual Death:

Spiritual death is the separation of the soul from God. The penalty proclaimed in Eden, which has fallen upon the race, is primarily this death of the soul (Gen. 2:17; Rom. 5:21; Eph. 2:1, 5) KJV; NIV; By it, man lost the presence and favour of God as well as the knowledge of and desire of God. Because of this, he needs to be made alive from death (Luke 15:32; John 5:24; 8:51; Eph. 2:5). KJV; NIV.

Eternal Death:

Eternal death is simply the culmination and completion of spiritual death. It is the eternal separation of the soul from God, together with the accompanying remorse and outward punishment.

(Matt. 10:28; 25:41; 2 Thess. 1:9; Heb. 10:31; Rev. 14:11) KJV; NIV This matter is external more fully in our study of future things of the Most High God. God reveals His plans to his people; His ways are eminent (sure).

The Bible says in Isaiah 55:6-8 (NIV), "Seek the Lord while he may be found, call on him while he is near." Vs. 7, Let the wicked forsake his way and the evil man his thoughts, let him turn to the Lord and he will have mercy on him, and to our God, for he will freely pardon.

Vs. 8, "For my thoughts are not your thoughts, neither your ways my ways," declares the Lord. His ways are not ours; therefore, it is the master's plan for believers to walk in his ways and his will for our lives.

The extent of Depravity: The Scripture speaks of human nature as wholly depraved. However, the doctrine of "total depravity" is easily misunderstood and misinterpreted. It is essential to know both what it means and what it does. From the negative standpoint, it does not mean that every sinner is devoid of all qualities pleasing to men; that he commits or is prone to every form of sin; or that he is bitterly exposed to God as men can be.

Jesus recognized the pleasing qualities in some individuals (Mark 10:21). KJV He said that the scribes and Pharisees did things God demanded. (Matt. 23:23) KJV Paul asserted that some Gentiles "do instinctively of the things of the law" (Rom. 2:14) KJV God told Abraham that the iniquity of the Amorites would grow worse (Gen. 15:16) KJV, and Paul said that "evil men and impostors will proceed from bad to worse" (2 Tim. 3:13) KJV

12. GOD'S GREAT COMMISSION FOR HIS PEOPLE:IS THE COMMAND TO "PRAY"

Matt. 28:19-20 KJV "Go ye therefore, and teach all nations, baptizing them in the name of the Father, and of the Son, and the Holy Ghost: Teaching them to observe all things whatsoever I have commanded you: and, lo, I am with you always, even unto the end of the world. Amen.

Mark 16:15-16 KJV "And he said unto them, Go ye into all the world and preach the gospel to every creature. He that believeth and is baptized shall be saved; but he that believeth not shall be damned.

PRAYER

_____
_____
_____
_____

13. TESTIMONIALS

Prophetess Winnie Smith is someone I have grown to admire. I met her roughly 6 years ago during a live broadcast. We later connected after the broadcast, and since then, she has been one of the mentoring voices in my life. Her passion for God's people and their souls is genuinely inspiring. Her faithful walk with God, her level of faith, and her belief in all of God's promises are enough to ignite faith in any struggling believer.

She has a pure heart; she gives and pours all of what she knows freely into anyone willing to sit at her feet and learn. She stands out as a prophet who runs after God's heart; her accuracy and ability to build, nurture, and teach are impeccable. Prophetess Winnie walks in integrity; she honours the leadership role and the voice she represents in the lives of those she mentors.

The Believer's Code is a book that will assist any believer in their walk with God. Its rich content will empower you, bringing clarity, knowledge, and understanding of your purpose. It is great for personal growth and development in your Christian walk. This book has truly blessed me, and I am confident it will bless you as well.

Carlie Louis

(Prophetess CeCe)

Founder of Unbreakable Women's Ministry

14. SCRIPTURES FOR NEW BELIEVERS

Matt. 11: 28-29 KJV

Come unto me, all ye that labour and are heavy laden, and I will give thee rest. Take my yoke upon you, and learn of me; for I am meek and lowly in heart: and ye shall find rest unto your soul.

Romans 6:23 KJV

For the wages of sin is death, but the gift of God is eternal life in Christ Jesus.

Romans 10:9 KJV

Because if you confess with your mouth that Jesus is Lord and believe in your heart that God raised him from the dead, you will be saved.

Hebrews 11:6 KJV

But without faith, it is impossible to please him: for he that cometh to God must believe he is and that he is a rewarder of them who diligently seek him.

Psalms 50:15 KJV

Call upon me in the day of trouble, I will deliver thee, and you will glorify me!

1 John 2:15 KJV

Love not the world, neither the things in the world; if any man loves the world, the love of the Father is not in him.

15. DAILY INSPIRING AFFIRMATIONS FOR YOU TO RECITE

- I affirm that Jesus is the Lord over my life.

- I affirm that I am a kingdom citizen, and I receive every good thing required to live a fulfilled and supernatural life.

- I affirm that I am the inheritance of my Father; therefore, I am blessed with all good treasures that my Father owns in Jesus' name.

- I affirm that I have God's life in me, that I do what the Father does, that His light illuminates through me, and that I am light in a dark place.

- I affirm that the sky's the limit; I think,

receive, talk, and walk big.

- I affirm that my faith in God propels me into magnitudes, making everything I have ever dreamed of limitless.

- I affirm that my body is ignited and strengthened to carry out God's divine order here on earth; Amen!

- I affirm that my Godly heritage will rest upon my generation now and those to come in Jesus' name!

- I affirm that through Jesus Christ dying on the cross for the redemption of my sins, I live and have been in Him. Giving God all the glory!

- I affirm that I am a magnet for soul-winning; I will share the gospel of Jesus Christ with the world until the day I leave this earth, keeping the faith in Jesus Christ.

- I affirm that Rom. 1:16 I am not

ashamed of the gospel of Jesus Christ, for it is the power of God unto salvation to everyone that believeth; to the Jews first, and also to the Greeks!

- I affirm that God is my protector from all fiery darts of the enemy; I walk with power and authority, looking to Jesus, the author and the finisher of my faith.

- I affirm that God's unmerited favour and grace will be in my life and the lives of my generation.

ABOUT THE AUTHOR

Prophetess Winnie M. Smith is a seasoned teacher, intercessor, and prophetic voice dedicated to equipping believers for victorious Christian living. Born into a lineage of prophetic heritage, she has walked in the supernatural from a young age, carrying a mantle of healing, deliverance, and revelatory knowledge.

For over two decades, Prophetess Winnie has served faithfully in church leadership, evangelism, mentorship, and deliverance ministry. Her life is marked by humility, compassion, and unwavering dedication to the Word of God. With a powerful testimony of endurance, obedience, and spiritual resilience, she has become a vessel God uses to strengthen the body of Christ and call believers back to biblical foundations.

Through her teaching, prayer ministry, and prophetic insight, Prophetess Winnie helps Christians understand their identity, embrace holiness, and walk in the fullness of God's intended purpose. *The Believer's Code* is her signature work — a culmination of her spiritual journey, doctrinal study, and divine assignment to build, restore, and prepare God's people for the end-time harvest.

She is a mother, mentor, servant-leader, and warrior for the Kingdom whose heart beats to see lives transformed through the power of Jesus Christ.

Winnie has a lot to share, that will propel your faith in Jesus Christ, great testimonies of the Goodness of GOD, him sending people in the work place, using her to pray for the sick, she has also prayed for the staff and her boss and his wife was healed form sickness, autism kid, Muslim man and woman was also prayed for, she explained when GOD send them in, she knows by the gifting of the HOLY SPIRIT, been sent on the road to specific places, hospitals, friend's home, knowing they were sick and needed healing, even when they didn't tell her, mom she was healed from Colon Cancer by her believing God for her mom, family members healed from Prostate Cancer.

Winnie is an Intercessor, a worshipper, and a teacher of the gospel of Jesus Christ. And

He gave some apostles, some prophets, some evangelists, some pastors, and some teachers. (Eph. 4:11) Called to the fivefold ministry; She is a certified and registered Chaplain in Ontario; humbled and receptive to His will.

Rhema Christian Ministries

"Biblical Studies"

Certificates 2009 & 2011

Canada Christian College

Bachelor of Theology Studies"

Year of: 2014-2017

Ordained Lay Evangelist in 2014

Christ Embassy Bayview

"Foundation School"

Christian Biblical Studies

2018……..Trophy Evangelist of the year 2018

Canadian Evangelical Association

Ordination: Pastor Winnie Smith

Year of: 2020

Gifts & Talents

Advanced Fashion Designer & Seamstress

The George Brown College Of Applied Arts and Technology F/T

Year of: 1981

Seneca College of Applied Arts and Technology

Pattern Drafting & Designing P/T

Year of: 1979

Contact information:

PAYMENTS, ORDERS & EMAILS: winnie.believerscode7@gmail.com

PH# Canada 1-(437) 991 7261

PH# Jamaica 1-(876) 783 0979

PH#2 Jamaica-1-(876) 839 5134

Paypal.me/Ws462

divakoutore@gmail.com

Faithful Prayers Global Ministries

Online ZOOM Meetings

ID: 988 613 1801

Psw: 266983

YOUTUBE LINK: winniesmithspeaksfaithfulp983